STRADBROKE DREAMTIME

KATH WALKER

Illustrated by
Lorraine Hannay

ANGUS
& ROBERTSON
PUBLISHERS

For my grandchildren,
Raymond and Petrina Walker

ANGUS & ROBERTSON PUBLISHERS

Unit 4, Eden Park, 31 Waterloo Road,
North Ryde, NSW, Australia 2113, and
16 Golden Square, London W1R 4BN,
United Kingdom

First published in Australia
by Angus & Robertson Publishers in 1972
Reprinted 1973
This re-illustrated edition 1982
Reprinted 1987

Copyright © Kath Walker 1972

National Library of Australia
Cataloguing-in-publication data.

Walker, Kath, 1920-
    Stradbroke dreamtime.

    Previously published: Sydney: Angus and Robertson,
    1972 with illustrations by Dennis Schapel.
    For children.
    ISBN 0 207 14770 1.

    [1]. Aborigines, Australian — Queensland — North
    Stradbroke Island — Juvenile literature.
    [2]. Aborigines, Australian — Legends — Juvenile
    literature. I. Hannay, Lorraine. II. Title.

994.3'20049915.

Printed in Hong Kong

Contents

Stories from Stradbroke

Stories from the Old and New Dreamtime

Kath Walker says~

These stories were written while I was staying at Tamborine Mountain, in Queensland, Australia, with the well-known Australian poet Judith Wright. It is a lovely place, the home of a thousand birds and animals, and Judith Wright helps to guard the mountain and its creatures from the greedy speculators who threaten to come there with mechanical shovels to dig it up and destroy it.

Ee–ee–ee–wheep–chooo–chooo! That is the call of the whipbird, in the garden at Tamborine Mountain. Sometimes I call out, "Hullo, Whippy!" He creeps up behind me and clearly says, "*I'm–m–m–m–chung . . . chung!*" I think he wants me to believe he can speak Chinese. He can't, you know. He's never been outside Australia.

Down in the gully at the end of the paddock, an old pheasant holds court with his wife. Every morning and evening he booms out his orders. On the other side of the house, a little butcher bird often taps against the window-pane. He's a clever one, that bird. He knows he will get fed if he looks sad enough. Then there is a beautiful, blue-eyed bower bird who never utters a word, just flies to the feeding-post, takes some bread and meat, and then goes off again. I think she seems rather disdainful, but Judith says she is really timid and shy.

Not long ago, a poor thin cow wandered into the garden, and now she lives there. Poor old cow is so thin you can easily count her ribs. Every time she takes a deep breath I find myself holding on to mine, because it looks as though the skin on her right side will meet up with the skin on her left side before she breathes out again. But she will soon fatten up in her new home.

There are lots of other creatures in this garden: bandicoots, possums, lizards, snakes. . . . While I was staying at Tamborine Mountain, it was my job to collect the eggs from the three plump hens in the fowl-run. I like eggs, and so does Waumpty Crow. He is a very clever, cheeky robber, and we spent a lot of time trying to outsmart each other. Sometimes he got to the eggs first, but most times I beat him to them. He would sit high on a tree branch, watching me with his bright, beady eyes, and he would caw: *Gaaarn–gaaarn–gaaarn!*

It was real Bunyip weather—damp and misty—for a lot of the time I was busy writing my stories. I have written about Bunyip in the second part of this book: you will find him in the Old and New Dreamtime stories. The first part of the book are stories I remembered about my childhood on Stradbroke Island, off the Queensland coast, where I lived with my Aboriginal family. I hope you will enjoy reading what I have written.

Stories from Stradbroke

Stradbroke

STRADBROKE, an island that was once stocked with natural beauty: the rocks of Point Lookout at the far end of the island, and the sea smashing its boiling foam against the rock base; ferns and flowers growing in abundance; the white miles of sand stretching as far as the eye could see, daily washed by the rolling Pacific Ocean.

Years ago, my family—my Aboriginal family—lived on Stradbroke Island. Years before the greedy mineral seekers came to scar the landscape and break the back of this lovely island. I recall how we used to make the trip to Point Lookout. My father would saddle our horses at early light and we would make our way along the shoreline, then cut inland to climb over the hills covered with flowering pines, wattles and gums. The brumbies would watch our approach from a safe distance. These wild horses never trusted man, their foe. They would nuzzle their foals, warning them to stay away from their enemy.

The shells washed up by the sea delighted us. Sometimes, too, we found strange, small-scale outrigger craft. Father told us that some of our neighbours to the north of Australia prayed to their god to bless their fishing fleet, and tossed these model ships into the sea to appease the waves.

There was one sight we loved above all others. When we arrived at Point Lookout, we would tether our horses out of sight, then take up position behind the small sandhills that dotted the shore. We would lie full-length upon our stomachs and silently wait for the beautiful nautilus shells to come out of the sea. They looked like little ships in full sail. Their trumpet-like shells would unfurl to the breeze a sail, mauve-coloured, which caught the sun's rays and shone like satin. We feasted our eyes upon the sight, knowing it would not last long, for at the least sound these shy creatures would immediately draw in their satin sails and drop like stones to the safety of the sea bottom.

The island is different now. Civilization and man's greed have chased away our shy nautilus shells. Motor-cars belch fumes over the land, and the noise of industry drowns out all other sounds of life. Men's machines have cut and maimed and destroyed what used to be.

Stradbroke is dying. The birds and animals are going. The trees and flowers are being pushed aside and left to die. Tourists come to soak up the sunshine and bathe in the blue Pacific, scattering as they go their discarded cans and cigarette packs and bottles and even the hulks of cars.

Greedy, thoughtless, stupid, ignorant man continues the assault on nature. But he too will suffer. His ruthless bulldozers are digging his own grave.

Kill to Eat

MY father worked for the Government, as ganger of an Aboriginal work-force which helped to build roads, load and unload the supply ships, and carry out all the menial tasks around the island. For this work he received a small wage and rations to feed his seven children. (I was the third-eldest daughter.) We hated the white man's rations—besides, they were so meagre that even a bandicoot would have had difficulty in existing on them. They used to include meat, rice, sago, tapioca, and on special occasions, such as the Queen's Birthday festival, one plum pudding.

Of course, we never depended upon the rations to keep ourselves alive. Dad taught us how to catch our food Aboriginal-style, using discarded materials from the white man's rubbish dumps. We each had our own sling-shots to bring down the blueys and greenies—the parrots and lorikeets that haunted the flowering gums. And he showed us how to make bandicoot traps; a wooden box, a bit of wire, a lever on top and a piece of burnt toast were all that was needed. Bandicoots cannot resist burnt toast. We would set our traps at dusk, and always next day there was a trapped bandicoot to take proudly home for Mother to roast. Dad also showed us how to flatten a square piece of tin and sharpen it. This was very valuable for slicing through the shallow waters; many a mullet met its doom from the accurate aim of one of my brothers wielding the sharpened tin. Dad made long iron crab hooks, too, and we each had a hand fishing-line of our own.

One rule he told us we must strictly obey. When we went hunting, we must understand that our weapons were to be used only for the gathering of food. We must never use them for the sake of killing. This is in fact one of the strictest laws of the Aborigine, and no excuse is accepted for abusing it.

One day we five older children, two boys and three girls, decided to follow the noise of the blueys and greenies screeching from the flowering gums. We armed ourselves with our sling-shots and made our way towards the trees.

My sisters and I always shot at our quarry from the ground. The boys would climb onto the branches of the gum-trees, stand quite still, and pick out the choicest and healthiest birds in the flock. My elder brother was by far the best shot of all of us. He was always boasting about it, too. But never in front of our mother and father, because he would have been punished for his vanity. He only boasted in front of us, knowing that we wouldn't complain about him to our parents.

The boys ordered us to take up our positions under the trees as quietly as possible. "Don't make so much noise!" they told us. In spite of the disgust we felt for our boastful brother, we always let him start the shooting. He was a dead shot, and we all knew it. Now we watched as he drew a bead on the large bluey straight across from him. The bird seemed intent on its honey-gathering from the gum-tree. We held our breath and our brother fired.

Suddenly there was a screeching from the birds and away they flew, leaving my brother as astonished as we were ourselves. He had been so close to his

victim that it seemed impossible he should have missed . . . but he had. We looked at him, and his face of blank disbelief was just too much for us. We roared with laughter. My other brother jumped to the ground and rolled over and over, laughing his head off. But the more we laughed, the angrier my elder brother became.

Then, seeming to join in the fun, a kookaburra in a nearby tree started his raucous chuckle, which rose to full pitch just as though he, too, saw the joke.

In anger my elder brother brought up his sling-shot and fired blindly at the sound. "Laugh at me, would you!" he called out. He hadn't even taken time to aim.

Our laughter was cut short by the fall of the kookaburra to the ground. My brother, horrified, his anger gone, climbed down and we gathered silently around the stricken bird. That wild aim had broken the bird's wing beyond repair. We looked at each other in frightened silence, knowing full well what we had done. We had broken that strict rule of the Aboriginal law. We had killed for the sake of killing—and we had destroyed a bird we were forbidden to destroy. The Aborigine does not eat the kookaburra. His merry laughter is allowed to go unchecked, for he brings happiness to the tribes. We call him our brother and friend.

We did not see our father coming towards us. He must have been looking for firewood. When he came upon us, we parted to allow him to see what had happened. He checked his anger by remaining silent and picking up a fallen branch. Mercifully he put the stricken bird out of its misery. Then he ordered us home.

On the way back we talked with awesome foreboding of the punishment we knew would come. I wished our father would beat us, but we all knew it would not be a quick punishment. Besides, Dad never beat us. No, we knew the punishment would be carefully weighed to fit the crime. When we got home, our mother was told to give us our meal. Nothing was said of the dead kookaburra, but we knew Dad would broach the subject after we had eaten. None of us felt hungry, and our mother only played with her food. We knew that Dad had decided upon the punishment, and that Mother had agreed to it, even if she felt unhappy about it.

It was our mother who ordered us to bring into the backyard our bandicoot traps, our sling-shots, and every other weapon we had. We had to place them in a heap in the yard, while our father carefully checked every item. Our big black dog stood with us. He always did that when there was trouble in the family. Although he could not possibly understand the ways of human beings, he could nevertheless interpret an atmosphere of trouble when it came.

Father spoke for the first time since we had killed the kookaburra. He asked for no excuses for what we had done, and we did not offer any. We must all take the blame. That is the way of the Aborigine. Since we had killed for the sake of killing, the punishment was that for three months we should not hunt or use our weapons. For three months we would eat only the white man's hated rations.

During those three months our stomachs growled, and our puzzled dog would question with his eyes and wagging tail why we sat around wasting our time when there was hunting to be done.

It happened a long time ago. Yet in my dreams, the sad, suffering eyes of the kookaburra, our brother and friend, still haunt me.

Shark

THE big black dog sat in the yard looking at the sea. The tide was out and the mud-flats were alive with sea-birds. Curlews were calling and the ibises walked with heads down, searching with their beaks for seaweed. Gulls fought each other on the sand-flats, and the mangrove Jack, crouched like a hunchback, pretended to sleep and waited for the small fish and crabs to venture too near him.

The dog was puzzled. Lately the pattern of life seemed to have changed. The little humans had gone to school, and the woman always seemed to be busy washing. He watched the little humans go off with their schoolbags each morning; he went with them as far as the bridge, but he was forbidden to go any farther. They would be gone for a long time. He was bored with just sitting around. This morning the mud-flats called him. He pretended not to hear and stretched himself full-length on the grass, and yawned. He wondered why the little humans no longer went hunting. They, too, seemed to sit and grow bored when they were home.

The curlew called to his mate on the mud-flat, and the dog pricked up his ears and made up his mind. He bounded through the fence and across the sand until he came to the low-water mark left by the tide. He watched the small toads darting to and fro in the shallows. With one paw raised he snapped at the toads, but it was only in fun. The little humans had trained him as a pup not to touch the toads. Now, his grown-up-dog instinct told him that if he swallowed a sea-toad it could poison him.

The black dog wandered farther into the water, where the long seaweed grew near the deepest part of the channel. His keen eyes watched for movement in the water. He knew this was the place of the salmon sharks. His mouth watered for the taste of shark. The little humans often took him with them in the dinghy when they hunted the small salmon sharks, which built their nests in the long seaweed. But they always made him stay in the boat, though he had tried hard to convince them that he was a match for any shark. In vain, for the smallest human always held him with her arms entwined round his neck. He could easily have broken away, but he would never disobey the little humans' commands.

The dog's eyes caught a movement in the seaweed. He froze, one paw raised, his mind wholly alert to the need to concentrate on the body of the shark, which he saw outlined against the slowly moving nest of seaweed. He sprang forward; his strong jaws snapped and caught the shark's tail. It was only half-grown, and in its panic to get away, it made the mistake of flicking its tail and darting against the outgoing tide. A full-grown shark would never have made such an error. The fish darted onto a half-submerged sandbank, realized its mistake, and struggled to free itself. But that error cost it its life. The dog pounced again. Grabbing the shark by the tail, he tossed his head and flicked the fish high and dry onto the mud-flat. Then he sat by the dying shark, catching his breath. He stood up and shook the water off his coat and out of his ears and eyes.

The dog tried to pick up the shark in his jaws, but it was too big for him. It was much bigger than the goannas, lizards and snakes he often carried home from the hunt with the little humans. They were not here to help him; he must find a way to carry the shark home. He looked towards the house. It was about a quarter of a mile away.

Finally he worked out a plan of action. Taking the now almost dead shark by the tail, he dragged it after him, stopping every now and then to take a rest. He dragged it as far as the beach gate, and decided that was far enough. Now, if he could persuade the woman to come out, she could carry it the rest of the way for him.

The dog barked and barked, but the woman took no notice. The dog dared not leave the shark and go to find the woman; another dog might come along and take it from him in his absence. So he sat up and gave the most pitiful howl he could muster.

That howl had the desired effect. The woman opened the house door to see what was wrong with the dog. When she saw the shark, she came down the steps and out of the gate. She shaded her eyes against the sun and looked out toward the drag marks on the sand, and realized what the dog had done. She patted his head and stooped to pick up the shark. The dog placed one paw on his prize.

"It's all right, boy. I know it's yours. I'll cook it for you. Hungry for fish, eh? Can't say I blame you. Better than that muck the white man calls food."

The dog whirled himself around and around, barking excitedly.

"Come on, then, you can keep your eye on it while it cooks."

The dog lay on a bran bag on the kitchen floor, sniffing every now and then at the appetizing smell of the cooking shark.

When the little humans returned from school, they too sniffed the smell of cooked shark and looked in amazement at each other, for it was not yet three months since they had shot at the kookaburra, and the hunting ban was still in force. The woman told them how the shark had come there, and they looked with envy at the dog. They sat and talked about it on the grass outside the house, until the woman came out with a large dish which she set down on the ground.

The dog wagged his tail and licked his chops.

"There's your shark, boy. Eat it up!"

He barked and ran from the dish to the little humans, trying to tell the woman that he wanted them to share the meal with him, but she shook her head. "No, boy, it's all yours. They cannot have any. Go on now—eat."

The dog did not understand, but he ate his fill while the little humans sat and watched him. After he had emptied the dish, he came and sat with them. His belly felt warm and happy again.

The smallest human took the dish inside, then came running out again. "Guess what we're having for tea," she said in disgust. "Tapioca and sago—*yuk*!"

The Tank

MY father was always on the lookout for the sort of things that would make life a bit easier for all of us. As there was never enough money to buy what was needed, we had to make the most of what we could find lying around—usually on the white man's rubbish dumps.

One day Dad came home from work with an old leaky water-tank tied to the dray. I well remember the old draught-horse that pulled the dray: property of the Government, of course. He looked as though he were always frothing over, hence his name—Soda. One of Dad's mates helped him unload the old tank, and when they had carried it round to the back of the house, Mother came out to inspect it.

"And what," she demanded, "will that leaky thing do for us?"

Dad's look told her to wait and see.

The next day Dad got to work. He built a tank-stand, and then all the family and friends he could muster helped him lift the tank onto the stand.

Mother placed her hands on her hips, the way she always did when Dad wouldn't explain to her just what he had in mind. "It's riddled with holes, it can't hold water, so what...." She raised her eyebrows as she awaited Dad's reply.

"I'm going to get some cement and fix up the inside. Then it'll hold water, won't it?" Dad told her.

"Not a bad idea," Mother said. "But how are you going to buy the cement? You're not exactly a millionaire, you know."

Her sarcasm was lost on Dad. He grabbed his hat and waved good-bye, warning us not to go near the so-and-so tank.

"Tank, is it!" Mother yelled after his retreating figure.

Dad never did anything unless he had first planned everything out in detail. He'd known about that discarded water-tank on the dump for a long time, but he'd waited until his holidays came round before he did anything about it, so that he could get on with the job without interruptions.

Later he returned with several bags of cement which he carried into our lean-to shed. Mother, who never approved of taking anything without paying our way, kept asking Dad how he had got the cement, and Dad kept pretending that he hadn't heard her questions.

"Your father can be very deaf when he feels like it," she remarked.

However, she got the message from his silence. There was a sort of code between our parents which they used when we kids were around. If Dad had come by something which he'd found or someone had given him, then he would answer Mother's questions. If, on the other hand, he had "borrowed" something that was really the property of the Government, then he just didn't answer her questions. Dad's philosophy was simple: if you really need something and can't afford to buy it, then you should take it. He never thought of this as wrong. It wasn't his fault that he never had much money. The fault lay with the Government, which doled out such low wages to Aborigines. We really needed a water-tank, and I know that if Dad had had the money to buy one, he would rather have done so.

14

Now, he got us all busy carrying the sand and gravel for mixing the cement. We kids always had to play our part in Dad's do-it-yourself schemes. As soon as the cement was ready, Dad placed a ladder against the tank. He climbed to the top, then, sitting on the edge of the tank, hoisted up the ladder and put it down inside. He then climbed down, and shouted to us to pull up the ladder and prop it up against the outside of the tank once more. We two older girls then had to take it in turns to climb the ladder and throw down all the tools he needed: hammer, chisel, pliers, nails, wire. . . . My youngest sister had the job of holding the ladder steady. When Dad thought he had everything he needed, my older sister and I were told to fetch the groceries from the store. My youngest sister was left to help Dad, in case there was anything else he might need thrown down to him.

Mother was busy cooking; she had lost all interest in Dad's cementing scheme by this time. Presently she called my youngest sister indoors and told her to set the table for lunch, so she came inside the house and started rattling the knives and forks.

Mother, looking out of the window, saw the ladder leaning against the tank. "Why can't people put things away after they've finished with them," she muttered.

She went outside and shifted the ladder to the place where it was always kept when not in use—under the house.

Meanwhile, my sister and I returned from our shopping expedition. We noticed the ladder was not against the tank any longer, and concluded that Dad had gone off somewhere. That was what my youngest sister thought, too, when she saw it had gone. Lunch was ready by now, and Mother called us all in to eat. Dad didn't appear, so she carefully placed his dish in the oven, remarking that it wasn't like him to go off without letting her know when he would be back.

After lunch we cleared the table and washed the dishes in no time flat, so that we could go off swimming. Mother, glad to get out of the hot kitchen, and with us out of the way for the afternoon, made for her bed. She lay down and gazed dreamily out of the window. First she saw a hammer sailing through the air, then a chisel, followed by lengths of wire, pebbles, nails, screws . . . . Dad was really emptying his tool-box.

Mother rose from her bed, wondering where all those things were coming from. Suddenly it dawned on her. Out she flew to the tank and knocked against its side. "Ted, is that you in there?" she asked.

Dad's voice was hoarse with the dust inside the tank. "No, it's a blasted bull-frog gone mad!" he yelled.

"All right, all right, don't you lose your temper with me," Mother warned him.

She ran down to the sea and called us out of the water. We soon had the ladder against the tank and managed to hand it to Dad so that he could climb out.

"Why the heck didn't you stay on the job as you were told?" he demanded of my younger sister.

"Mum told me to get the table ready for lunch," she explained.

Dad raised his eyes expressively. "That's the trouble around this place. Too many bosses!"

Mother wisely ignored this remark.

Dad went on with the job next day, but he kept the ladder inside the tank with him, and it stayed there until he wanted to come out again.

When the rains came and filled the tank, we revelled in the luxury of laid-on water.

Where's Mother?

MY sister and I were playing on the beach by the creek. The dirt road ran alongside the beach for a quarter of a mile, before it turned left and lost itself in the bush foliage. We had spent the afternoon playing games with some white children who had camped by the creek. Their grandmother, every year, gathered them up for this camping holiday away from the busy life of the city on the mainland. These children fitted in very well with the Aboriginal community, and a firm friendship had grown between them and the Aboriginal tribe.

I looked up at the sky. "I wonder why Mother hasn't called us home yet," I thought. "It's nearly sunset."

The sky was changing from blue to dusky pink. Idly I watched the beach road. I saw a figure dressed in pink disappearing out of sight, around the bend. Pink, like the sunset clouds . . . .

"Don't you think it's funny, Mum not calling us home?" I asked my sister. She shrugged.

"You know what?" I went on. "I think I saw Mum going along the road just now in her best pink dress."

"Don't be silly," my sister said. "Mum's at home."

"I'm sure it was her."

"Mum wouldn't go away from home without telling us," she replied.

"You wait here," I told her. "I'll go home and find out if she's still there."

I left her on the beach while I went home. I searched the yard, the fowl-run, even the lavatory, then went inside the house. Dad was resting on the bed, reading a newspaper. He looked at me over his glasses.

"What did you come home for, girl?" he asked.

I could tell from the way he asked the question that he had not reckoned on my coming home.

"Oh, I came to put the oars away," I replied. I could always find a convincing answer to any question in an emergency. I sensed now that we were being tricked by some plot that Mum and Dad had thought up together, so it didn't really bother me that I had told Dad a lie. I left Dad to his newspaper and came back to my sister.

"Well?" she asked.

"Mum's not home," I told her.

She couldn't believe it. In all our life we had never known Mother leave home by herself, without taking one or other of us with her. My sister was six years old at this time; I was a year older.

"I know that was Mum I saw in the pink dress, going down the road," I told my sister. "She must have gone off to a concert or something without taking us or even telling us where she was going. She must have asked the white woman to keep her eye on us." I had remembered that there was a concert on that night at our community hall.

"That's right—we were told we must play with the other kids and not go away. It's getting dark, and we haven't had tea yet. Was the table set in the kitchen for tea?"

I shook my head. "The tablecloth wasn't even spread."

"Then we must be going to have tea with the other kids." My sister sounded really puzzled. "Why would Mum go off by herself like that? Without Dad, even?"

"Oh, she's often left Dad at home before, but she's never left us," I told her. "I think we should walk over to that concert hall and find Mum."

"What about our tea?"

"I don't feel hungry. Do you?"

"No-oo. I did before, but I don't now."

I took hold of my sister's hand. "Come on, let's find Mum."

She held back. "Shouldn't we let them know we're going?"

I glanced towards the other children and their grandmother. "No," I replied firmly. "They'd stop us going. We won't tell anyone."

So we set off for the community hall, a wooden building with an iron roof that was about five miles away. I led the way along the dirt track we called a road. It was dark and I felt frightened. I wondered whether the big bull was out of his paddock. We half ran, half walked the distance, and at last the lights of the hall came into view. We went up to the open door. The hall was packed; even the doorway was filled with men standing to watch the show. The women were all seated on chairs inside the hall.

I was sure that Mum was sitting in there. Determined to find her, I tugged sharply on the coat of one of the men in the doorway. He turned round and looked down in astonishment at us. We stared up at him. He looked at our dirty dresses, untidy hair and bare feet, then cleared a path for us through the men standing beside him.

I just managed to take in the fact that a magician was performing tricks on the stage as the man who had made way for us called softly to the beautiful woman sitting on one of the chairs, looking happy and relaxed in her pretty pink dress.

"Hey, Lucy, look here."

Mother turned and saw us. Shock and amazement spread over her face, then she quickly grabbed her handbag and made her way out of the hall.

"Good grief, where did you come from? Just look at your dirty faces and your clothes! How did you get here?" she asked.

"We walked," I told her.

"Sometimes we ran, too," my sister said.

My mother sighed. "Come on, we're going home."

"Can't we watch the concert with you?" I asked hopefully.

"In that state? I'd be ashamed to sit down beside you. No, we're going home. You've spoilt my whole evening." Mother sounded sad as well as cross.

As we neared home, we saw that the whole place was in an uproar. Torches and lanterns were bobbing about all over the place. Men, women and children were searching the mud-flats at low-water mark, the mangroves and the bracken ferns. The old white grandmother was standing on the beach holding a carbide lamp high in the air. She was busy watching the search when we arrived back with

Mother. The old lady was so relieved to see my sister and me safe and sound that at first she simply could not think what to say. She picked up a tin cowbell which she used to summon her straying grandchildren when they were out swimming, and rang it loud and long to let the searchers know we had been found. This helped her to recover her composure. Then she exploded.

"You naughty, naughty girls, running away like that! You almost gave me a heart attack. I know your mother will punish you—and you thoroughly deserve it!"

When we got home and were finally packed off to bed, my sister fell asleep as soon as her tired head hit the pillow. I lay there counting the stars blinking at me through the open window. I heard my mother and father arguing in the next room. I knew that Mum was telling Dad off for not keeping an eye on us.

"For the first time in my life I get a chance to have a break away from the children, and look what happens." Mother talked in a low voice so as not to wake the children. It sounded like a one-sided argument to me. "Don't just lie there and pretend you can't hear me," Mother went on.

The squeak of springs meant that Father had turned his back on her in the hope that she would stop talking. She didn't.

"Leave it be, woman," he said finally. "Leave it be."

Silence filled the house at last. I went on counting the stars until I too fell asleep.

19

Going Crabbing

DAD believed in equality of the sexes, especially where work was concerned. If there was a job Dad wanted done, it didn't matter which of his children was closest—that one could do it. Mother never did go along with this idea; she was always complaining about him taking my sisters and me away from women's work. We girls were taught to paint sheds, and build them, too; chop wood; carry cans of water; fix the two-cylinder Wilson engine on our boat; cork the leaks in the dinghy; and carry out any other job that needed doing around the place. In fact, we did most of the work. The boys were more expert in being elsewhere when Dad decided to get a job done.

One day Dad decided it was time to go look for mud-crabs once more. So that

night Mother set the alarm-clock for three the next morning, as she always did when we were going crabbing. Before sunrise next day we girls were ordered to show a leg almost before the alarm had stopped ringing.

I wouldn't recommend a walk on the mud-flats, carrying gear in the form of fishing-lines, bran bags, crab hooks, petrol and the tucker-box at half past three in the morning. I never liked it, because I was always half asleep, and because the mud-flats between our house and the boat would be almost covered with small soldier-crabs, which came out of their holes in the sand when the tide went out. Soldier-crabs are about the size of a walnut, pale-blue and yellow, and they look just like an army of marching soldiers. Even when I was wide awake, I used to watch my step, for the last thing I wanted to do was to squash a poor, innocent soldier-crab, in spite of the fact that they were such a nuisance on the flats. I always got very upset when I stood on them. My sisters thought I was crazy. They just put their feet down and expected the soldier-crabs to get out of their way. If they didn't—well, it was just too bad. Even Dad had a silent contempt for my sentiment. I could sense it. He prided himself on bringing up his children

tough but not brutal. My brothers and sisters were very strong, healthy, and logical. But I was weak and sentimental.

My father was proud of the fact that he was a third-generation sailor. The locals reckoned you could count the barnacles growing on his face. They used to call him Old Barnacle. He certainly knew and respected the sea. I've seen him sit in the cabin of our boat and tell us immediately the tide or the wind was changing. He seemed to smell the change coming.

Although all his children had a great love for the sea, none of us really understood her as Dad did. I remember his disgust when he realized I was unable to take to sailing as well as the others. Believe it or not, I had the audacity to get seasick every time I took to a boat.

My father would shake his head and say to Mother, "Three generations of sailors' blood in her veins, and just look at her contaminating the sea by spewing all over it!"

Mother, I think, was glad one of her children did not take too kindly to the sea. She came from inland, and was always a bit scared herself in a boat. She used to get sick, too. But such was her love for and faith in my father, and her pride in his sailing skill, that she never worried too much about him, even on a stormy night when he might be overdue back home. She would just light a hurricane lantern and place it in the window to help guide him home. Dad, natural sailor that he was, never failed to bring his boat and family safely back to port.

On those early-morning excursions to get mud-crabs, I could sometimes really enjoy the boat trip, so long as the sea was calm. We would hug the coastline of the island for several miles, and by the time we reached our destination, the sun would be just coming up over the horizon. There is something unfailingly and breathtakingly beautiful about a sunrise—and this was especially true of a sunrise over Stradbroke Island. The fantastic, indescribable light that brightened the sky always made me feel I was in the presence of the Good Spirit. The colours would appear in the sky as if from nowhere and blend together as the sun peeped over the horizon. It was like a great rainbow rolled up in a huge ball, covering the eastern sky. This spectacle never failed to move me, and before the last of the colours left the sky, I had always forgiven my father for getting me out of bed at such an early hour to go crabbing.

Our boat with its chugging two-cylinder engine would finally bring us to our destination, the place where the mud-crabs lurked. We had been through the crabbing drill so many times that there was never any need for Dad to give us orders. As we three girls stepped out of the boat onto the mud-flats, my younger sister would seize one bran bag and throw another to me, while my older sister took up the crab hook, which we needed for the crabs that had to be winkled out from beneath the roots of the mangrove-trees. Dad would stay on the boat and follow after us as we worked the flats. He would never permit us to bring aboard a ginny—a female crab. If we did, he would make us take it back again. We would gather enough crabs to feed the tribe, and no more, and we only went crab gathering about once every three months.

There were always plenty of crabs for the picking then. It is not so now. Man's greed and his careless upsetting of the natural balance of life have almost wiped out the mud-crabs of Stradbroke.

The Left-hander

I WAS left-handed. This was something that just didn't seem to matter one way or the other . . . until I went to school. Then I soon realized that the education department in those days considered it wrong for a child to write or sew with the left hand. There were many painful scenes when I refused to pick up a pencil with my right hand; many times the head teacher's ruler came down in full force on the knuckles of my left hand. I had to give in and write as best I could with my right hand. But for a long time I managed to hide from the sewing teacher the fact that I used my left hand for needlework.

When the sewing teacher picked up my piece of needlework to start off the sewing, she would begin with the needle and thread held in her right hand, sewing from right to left. Then she would hand the sample to me to continue the work, believing that I would sew in the same way. It didn't take me long to discover that by simply turning the work around, I could sew from left to right with my left hand.

I was always very careful to make sure no one saw what I was doing. I used to keep my head down and hold the piece of work below the desk while I sewed. I was good at needlework, and the teacher knew I could always be relied upon to turn in a good sample. She used to praise my work.

All went well until one morning when I sat as usual in the needlework class with my head bent over my sample. I longed to be outside in the hot sunshine. I heard the March flies buzzing against the window-panes, trapped like me inside the schoolroom. They would fly in on the wind, and were never able to get out again. My mind recalled the time when I once went to the window and tried to open it to free the flies, but the head teacher ordered me back to my seat and demanded to know why I had got up without permission. I couldn't explain. None of the white teachers would have understood. I just stared back at him, and he told me I was sullen and stubborn.

As my hands guided the needle from left to right, I dreamed about the world outside. I could hear the screeching of the blue mountain parrots calling and calling, trying to entice me out there . . . . I thought of my little dinghy and my fishing-line, and the places where I could dig the fat sand worms that the large whiting could not resist as they came swimming on the incoming tide. I thought, another twenty minutes and I shall be free to run the mile home. By then, the tide will be just right for catching the big whiting.

I did not notice that the sewing teacher had left her table and was standing by me. Suddenly, two white hands were placed firmly on my desk. My mind was wrenched from dreams of fishing. I fixed my startled gaze on the small watch on the teacher's wrist.

"Look at me," the teacher demanded.

I raised my eyes, then quickly dropped my gaze.

"You know you are forbidden to sew with your left hand!" the teacher told

me in a loud, angry voice. "How long have you been cheating me like this? You are a very stubborn, naughty girl!"

I could feel the eyes of all the other children turned full upon me. The teacher went on scolding me; she made me feel ashamed, then embarrassed—and at last very angry. I set my jaw, dropped my needlework sample on the floor, and brought my balled fists onto the desk.

"Don't you dare clench your fists like that," the teacher said.

But I no longer cared what she said. I looked at my left hand, tightly clenched. It was always getting me into trouble. Suddenly I raised my left fist and smashed it down on the shiny face of the teacher's watch. I felt the wetness of blood. There was blood on the teacher's hand. Was it all my blood, I wondered.

The teacher gave a cry of pain and quickly withdrew her hands. She turned and fled from the classroom.

Presently, the head teacher came in. I had to walk the length of the shocked schoolroom. I stood silently before him as he flicked his cane. He caned me six times on each hand. I thought, my father will get a letter. It will demand payment for the broken wrist-watch. Yes, they will make him pay for the damage I have done.

Carpet Snake

HE was a beauty, that ten-foot carpet snake we had as a pet. My father belonged to the Noo-muccle tribe of Stradbroke Island, and the carpet snake was his totem. He made sure he looked after his blood-brother. My mother belonged to a different tribe. The carpet snake was not her totem. She hated old Carpie, because of his thieving ways. She was proud of her fowl-run and of the eggs our hens provided. Carpie liked the fowl-run too; every time he felt hungry he would sneak in, select the choicest fowl in the run, and swallow it. He could always outsmart Mother, no matter what she did to keep her chooks out of his ravenous belly. But, somehow, Mother never was game enough to bring down the axe on Carpie's head. We all knew she was often tempted to do just that. I think two things stopped her: her deep respect for the fact that Dad's decisions were final around the house, and the thought that if she killed in anger, Biami the Good Spirit would punish her.

We all loved Carpie except for Mother—and the dog. The dog kept well out of Carpie's way, because he was scared stiff of him. He seemed to know that a ten-foot carpet snake can wind itself around a dog and swallow it whole.

One day Mother went away for a short while to hospital. She came home with a brand-new baby sister for us. The day of her homecoming, we were rather overawed as we watched the baby sleeping in her cot. The big black dog looked at the baby, too, and obviously approved of the new arrival. After a while, Mother shooed us out to play, placed the cover gently over the sleeping baby, and went to make herself a cup of tea. Some friends, tribal neighbours, called to welcome her home; playing in our summer-house of tea-tree bark that Dad had built to catch the cool breezes blowing from the bay, we heard the women gossiping and the clink of teacups. When the neighbours left, Mother peeped in with pride on her new baby.

Suddenly we heard Mother's voice raised in a terrible screech as she raced outside, calling to Dad. Dad read the urgency of that screech, dropped his hammer, and ran.

Mother looked as though she were having a fit. She was jumping up and down, running to snatch up the long-handled broom, swearing like a bullocky. We knew something terrible must have happened for Mother to carry on like this. She behaved differently in different sorts of emergencies. We knew this one was serious.

"Stop shouting, woman!" Dad ordered. "What's wrong?"

Mother pointed a shaking finger towards the bedroom. "Get that gluttonous reptile out of my bedroom!"

Dad went into the bedroom. There, curled up in the cot with the baby, now wide awake and crying, was old Carpie.

Carpie seemed to sum up the situation in no time flat. He quickly slithered off the bedclothes, down onto the floor and out of the door.

The dog was trying to do the right thing by the family, taking menacing steps towards the snake and making growling noises in his throat. He was very happy to obey Dad, however, when he called him off.

Finally Mother found her composure, once Carpie had disappeared. "But you mark my words, you stubborn fellow, that snake could have swallowed my baby," she told Dad.

"Don't be silly, woman, why would he want to swallow your baby when he can swallow your chooks any time he wants to?" Dad retorted, and shot out of the door before Mother could think up a reply.

After that old Carpie carried on exactly as before, roaming about the house wherever he pleased. He went on stealing fowls and eggs, and slept anywhere he liked—though he never again tried to get into my baby sister's cot. I used to like it when I went off to the lavatory and found him holed up there. He would stretch himself right out across a beam in the ceiling. I used to sit in the lavatory for hours and tell him my innermost secrets, and it was very satisfying the way old Carpie would never interrupt the conversation or crawl away. Mother often accused me of dodging chores by going off and spending such a long time in the lavatory. This wasn't quite true; all I wanted to do was to share my secrets with Carpie.

When Dad died, we lost Carpie. He just seemed to disappear. We never found out what happened to him. Perhaps Biami the Good Spirit whispered to him: "Your blood-brother has gone to the shadow land. Your days are numbered. Get lost."

I like to think he still roams somewhere. Maybe he found a better fowl-run. I hope so. Funny thing about women. When my father died and Carpie disappeared, Mother decided to give away her fowl-run. She seemed to lose interest in it, somehow.

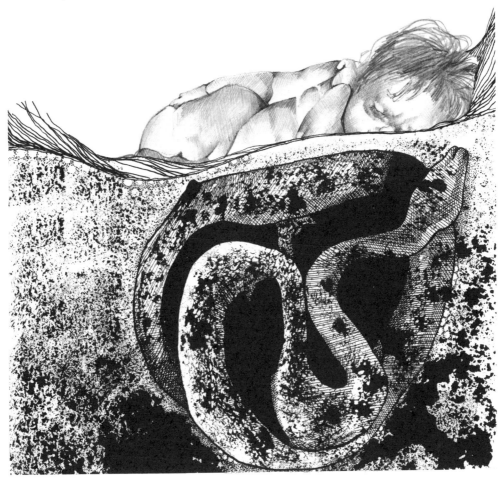

Family Council

THE family was holding one of its many council meetings. This time the grievance committee was airing its views. My two sisters and brothers were complaining that I did not pull my weight when it came to bringing home the food supplies from the hunt. They could all boast of a high tally of birds and animals they had brought home for the family larder. Although I always went hunting with them, I never did any good with my sling-shot and bandicoot traps. They said I spent too much time dreaming, or gathering flowers, or looking for discarded feathers, or drawing trees and animals and birds in the sand. That never made any sense to them, because the water always came and washed away my efforts with the receding tide. If I wasn't doing these things, then they complained that I'd go tramping off through the bush.

They were right. I never did take home any birds or animals for the larder. However, I did try to make up for my bad hunting record in other ways.

My eldest brother was allowed to make the first complaint against me. "She shouldn't be allowed to eat the food we bring home," he said. "She goes barging into the swamps and clumps of bushes just when I get a line on an extra-choice fat bird—and then I miss it because my stupid sister has warned it of our presence."

My second brother said darkly, "I think she gets up early and beats us to the bandicoot traps to let the creatures out."

My elder sister chipped in now. "She won't even help to carry home the bandicoots or birds when we do catch them."

My younger sister was not to be left out. "She deliberately puts Spitfire into her bandicoot trap to chase away the bandicoots. That cat of hers is wild—just like her! None of us can get anywhere near Spitfire except for her. She has it trained to frighten us away."

When my father finally asked me to speak, I didn't have much to say. All I could answer was that although it was true I didn't catch any game, it was quite untrue that I ever deliberately barged in to chase it away. Sometimes I just forgot about the need to keep still and quiet. And though I had a habit of getting up earlier than the others, I never released the bandicoots out of the traps. As for my younger sister, she was talking through her hat. I always set my bandicoot trap in just the same way as everyone else, but each time I went to see if I'd caught a bandicoot in it, I always found my cat in the trap instead. And it was, in fact, Spitfire that my brother had seen me releasing from the trap one morning, not a bandicoot! I had nothing to say to answer my elder sister's complaint that I would not carry the dead birds and animals home. I simply told my father straight out that I didn't like to do that.

Father was our arbitration judge. The rules were simple. Either we agreed with his decision, or we unanimously opposed it and appealed for another hearing. Having listened to the complaints and my defence, it was now his job to overrule the plaintiffs, if he could. I certainly hadn't been much help to him.

He turned to my brothers and sisters. "Who catches the most fish, and goes fishing most often of all of you?"

They had to admit that I was the best fisherman in the family.

"And who is best at crab spotting and catching?" my father went on.

Again they admitted that it was me.

"And the shellfish—how often is this gathered, and who spends most time filling the bags with it?"

Yes, they agreed that I did.

"So," said my father, "your sister has earned her place at the table. Even a fisherman must eat in order to fish."

There were never any more complaints against me after this. The others accepted the fact that they would have to put up with my bad hunting, and that I would never change. So I went on fishing, looking for crabs, and gathering shellfish—and I went on collecting fallen feathers, ferns and flowers while my brothers and sisters worked hard to bring home the rest of the game.

Repeat Exercise

Old Mac, the head teacher, was correcting a pile of exercise books. Sitting below his desk in the schoolroom, I watched as his pen crossed the paper. I tried to see whether it was my book he was busy with. When at last the books were given out, I opened mine and saw these words written in bold red ink across my homework: *Very bad, careless writing. Repeat exercise!*

I sighed, but I was not surprised. I was a very bad writer. My sisters and brothers were all good at writing, but I often had to repeat my exercises. My writing had been much better, before the teacher stopped me using my left hand.

That night, as I sat at the table at home with my two sisters, busy with homework, I looked at the hateful red writing in my exercise book and began to do last night's exercise all over again.

My elder sister had finished her homework and was peeling a banana. I envied her; she never seemed to have any trouble with schoolwork. She looked down at my book.

"Got another repeat?" she asked.

"I always get repeats," I growled. "You wouldn't like to do it for me, would you?"

She took a bite of banana. "What's it worth?"

"I'll give you a penny."

My sister pulled a face. "Not enough."

"Twopence?"

She shook her head.

"Threepence."

She took another bite of banana, and smirked.

"All right. You know I've only got sixpence to my name. You can have it if you can disguise your handwriting to look like mine, only a bit neater."

My sister thought for a while, then picked up the exercise book and studied my bad writing. "Where's the money?" she asked.

"Can you really disguise your writing so that old schoolie Mac won't know it's yours?" I asked anxiously.

"Easy," my sister answered confidently.

Soon she had finished writing out the exercise, and as she handed back the book she pocketed my sixpence.

Next day, when old Mac saw the rewritten exercise in my book, he looked long and hard at the writing, then called me out of the class.

"This is not your writing," he told me sternly. "Who wrote out the exercise for you?"

I refused to answer. I looked at the floor and remained silent. Then he called my elder sister to his table.

"Did you write out this exercise for your sister?" he asked, pointing to the book.

31

She saw no point in denying it, and admitted that she had done it. We were both caned for our deceit, and old Mac wrote right across the page in my exercise book in his bright-red ink: *Done by someone other than the owner of this book. Repeat!*

I returned to my desk filled with the humiliation of being found out. I had lost not only my precious sixpence, but also my right to be trusted. That red writing seemed to burn a hole in my mind. Yet what could I possibly do about my bad exercises? If I wrote them myself I always got repeats, and if I paid someone else to do them I got into trouble—and I still had to repeat them. I was really ashamed of the red writing in my book. It worried me far more than old Mac could ever imagine. I did try to write neatly, but somehow I just found it impossible. If only he would let me use my left hand instead of my right, I was sure I could turn in a neat exercise.

I did not like to think what my father would say if he found out how we had tried to cheat over my repeat exercise. That night, as I sat down to my homework, I hid the new red writing with my forearm as I began to copy out the exercise on the opposite page; I came to the conclusion that the only thing to do was to finish up that book as quickly as possible and throw it away before he had a chance to look at it. There would be plenty of sentences written in red ink in the next book—that was sure—but not the dreadful words that proclaimed our deceit.

I picked up my pen and wrote out the exercise again, and this time I did not take any pains over it at all. I knew perfectly well that my plan would mean I had to do more and more homework, but the sooner I filled the book, the better. Anyway, maybe if I went on scribbling and not caring, old Mac would get tired of putting *"Repeat!"* on every page.

My sister looked over my shoulder and gasped. "That's terrible writing! You'll get a repeat for sure."

I didn't answer, but I thought fiercely: "I hope I do. I sure hope I do."

And my sister, looking sympathetic, quietly left me alone at the table.

Mumma's Pet

DAD had built a billy-goat cart for us. Dad always built things to last, and this was a sturdy, heavy construction. It consisted of two large bicycle wheels and a wooden-box frame. It looked like a large box on wheels, and had two shafts protruding from it.

We used the cart for all sorts of carrying jobs. One of us—usually me—would back into the cart like a billy-goat, take hold of the shafts, and pull while the others pushed from behind. When the cart wasn't in use for some labouring job or other, we children often played with it. Our garden was covered with buffalo grass, which tends to creep over everything in its way. As we lived so near the swamp marshes, it grew quick, green and abundant. We became expert at racing the billy-goat cart over the grass, especially where small dirt mounds, grass-grown, stuck above the ground. It didn't matter how roughly we treated that cart, it took all our punishment; Dad's carpentering was so thorough that it didn't even lose a nail.

One day my sisters and I decided to play with the cart by ourselves. My elder sister often showed resentment of my younger sister; she used to call her "Mumma's pet"—it was true that Mother was inclined to make more of a fuss of my younger sister, and as a result she was a bit spoilt. Today, however, we were playing happily together, good friends for once. My elder sister decided on a new game. She thought it would be fun to put our younger sister in the cart and for me—as usual—to be the billy-goat while she pushed from behind.

We were going great and my younger sister was yelling with excitement, while my elder sister ordered me to pull my weight and stop being lazy. I wasn't being lazy; I was putting all I could into pulling the cart, but it was a puny effort compared to my elder sister's unlimited strength. Carried away by the excitement of the game, my elder sister tried to get more effort out of me by pushing harder. We were going around and over the tops of the bumpy grass tussocks when suddenly my puny strength gave out, I lost my balance, and the cart tipped over.

My younger sister went sprawling over the side of the cart as I tried to regain my balance—but the cart was too heavy for me, and as she fell, one wheel came down on her outstretched arm, I fell on top of her and my elder sister fell on top of me. Our younger sister let out a yell of pain. She always did that whether she was hurt or not.

Finally we got ourselves sorted out, and righted the cart. Our younger sister was holding her arm and whimpering. My elder sister told her to stop play-acting. We knew how good she was at putting on an act—she never succeeded in impressing us the way she did Mother. Now, still holding her arm and whimpering, she said, "I'm going to tell Mum! You hurt me!"

"Oh, why don't you grow up, Mumma's little pet?" my elder sister retorted furiously. "Don't be such a cry-baby!"

"You did hurt me," my younger sister whimpered.

"All right, so we hurt you. Well, that means you have the right to hurt us back. That's fair, isn't it? You can hit us as hard as you like, provided you don't tell Mum what happened."

So my younger sister walloped into both of us with the arm that hadn't been hurt. "Take that!" she kept yelling as she hit us again and again.

My elder sister winced in mock pain, and cried out for my younger sister to go easy and not hit so hard. She was a great ham actor herself.

We decided to put the cart back in the toolshed and go indoors. My younger sister dragged along behind us, not speaking to us.

During the evening meal my elder sister and I watched her out of the corners of our eyes, wondering whether she would squeal on us. We didn't really trust her in spite of the pact we'd made. But my mother noticed that her youngest daughter was eating very little, and was strangely silent. Her face had a strained expression, too. At last Mother called her to the head of the table, and looked across at Dad.

"Ted," she said, "this girl looks sick to me."

Dad looked at his youngest daughter. "Come here, girl," he ordered.

He ran his hand gently down the arm she had half lifted; it looked stiff against her body. She suddenly gave a scream of pain. It sounded genuine all right. My other sister and I exchanged glances.

"Mum, this girl's arm is broken, I think," Dad said.

"How did it happen?" Mum asked our sister, but she just looked towards us with pained eyes, while we stared back at her with vacant expressions.

Dad summed up the situation fast. "All right," he said, turning to my elder sister, "what have you been up to? How did this girl get hurt?"

My elder sister blurted out the story of the billy-goat cart. "We were only playing together," she finished lamely.

"Well," Dad said, "she's got a broken arm as a result of your playing, and how are we to get her to a doctor? You know the doctor here only attends to white people—he doesn't treat Aborigines." Dad was really angry.

Mother cuddled our younger sister and made soothing noises as Dad gave out orders to our brothers. "Row out to the channel and see if there's a boat that will take her to a doctor on the mainland. Let's hope there's a decent white man out there."

My brothers ran off to the dinghy, and they did find a white man who came to the rescue. He placed his auxiliary yacht, *Flockwing*, at Dad's disposal, and I acted as Dad's offsider on the boat. We set sail with a stiffening breeze blowing and a storm brewing in the west. During the trip the weather turned very rough, but luckily the engine kept going. My sister's condition worsened during the trip, and she was violently ill. When we reached the mainland, the doctor there put her in hospital for the night. She was suffering from shock and seasickness as well as her broken arm.

What happened to my elder sister and me? We got the hiding of a lifetime from Mum—and when she was angry, she could wallop good and hard.

When my younger sister returned from the mainland, she was treated as a v.i.p.—both Mum and Dad spoilt her rotten. She took full advantage of this situation. My elder sister and I kept out of her way as much as possible during her convalescence. After her arm healed, everything returned to normal. But we never asked her to join in any games with the billy-goat cart again.

Not Our Day

WE were in the boat on our way home from the islands at the southern end of Stradbroke. It was a cold winter's day, and a stiff northerly wind was making conditions worse. The white resident farmers on those small islands grew fruit and vegetables for the Brisbane market, and Dad used to visit them about once a month to buy our stock of produce from them. We paid about five shillings for a sugar-bag full of fruit or vegetables. The farmers were almost as poor as our Aboriginal tribe. We had many friends among them.

It was a funny thing, Dad always picked a day to buy vegetables when we girls had made other plans. We specially hated leaving home on a Saturday; that was the day when we ironed our best clothes and prepared for the weekly picture-show in the evening.

We were growing up, and my two sisters and I were beginning to realize that boys were not just the crazy, lazy, insolent pests we used to think they were. We would discuss among ourselves which boy we liked best, trying not to let Dad know what we were talking about. Come to think of it, though, I don't think we fooled him one bit. I guess he must have noticed before we did that we were growing up fast.

That particular afternoon, we were sitting at the stern of the boat. My elder sister was steering, and Dad was sitting, as he always did, straight in front of the cabin so that he could watch the engine. When we were in the boat he seldom gave orders, but taught us to obey hand and head signals. My job was to watch him all the time and relay any message to my sister at the tiller. Our younger sister usually buried herself in a comic-book. We were able to talk quite freely at the stern of the boat if we wanted to; Dad couldn't hear us because of the noise of the engine. Now, we were trying to decide what dresses we would wear to the picture-show that evening. My elder sister was worried about the time. Dad had spent too long talking to the farmers, who always looked forward to Dad's visits, and to hearing news from his part of the world. Cut off as they were, they welcomed anyone who came to their farms.

We never carried a clock on board, and none of us had a watch. Dad depended on the sun's position in the sky. However, this afternoon my sister was feeling too independent to ask him what time he thought it was. She and Dad had got into an argument about something that morning. She studied the sun herself; it was now well over to the west, and she decided it was later than we thought. She doubted whether we would get home before dark. I never believed for one moment she could tell the time by the sun the way Dad could, but I was as anxious as she was to get home.

The tide was ebbing and the water could be misleading at such a time. What looked like deep water could suddenly reveal itself as a sandbank, unless you were careful to watch the flow of the tide. My sister was no novice to the tiller. Dad had taught us all how to steer, and how to avoid the sandbank traps. Today, however, she was so anxious to get home that she decided she could short-cut

the trip in spite of the ebbing tide. She took note of the tell-tale lightness of the sunken sandbank ahead of us, made a snap judgement, and decided to steer the boat straight across it instead of around it. She thought there was enough water between the bottom of the boat and the sunken bank.

Dad still had his gaze fixed on the engine when the boat hit the sandbank. The engine revved and threshed, throwing Dad forward, and the propeller roared its disapproval by churning up the sand. My sister held hard to the tiller and Dad moved towards the engine to put her into reverse. He didn't move fast enough. She conked out. Dad chewed his moustache, took off his hat, threw it on the floor, and flared at my sister.

"What the hell do you think you were doing?" he said as he climbed into the cabin.

My younger sister and I went overboard fast. The water was freezing cold, but somehow we didn't seem to notice it. With the tide ebbing we knew we could be stuck there all night if we didn't float her off. My elder sister raced to the bow and put all her strength into pushing, and we eventually managed to refloat the boat into deeper water, where my younger sister threw over the anchor and paid out as much line as we carried.

Dad took stock of the situation. "Now the engine's conked out, we'll be stranded here if we can't start her up," he told us. He looked at the sun and the ebbing tide and made a calculation. "We've about twenty minutes of water left under us, so find those flaming springs," he told us.

Whenever the boat hit a bank, the springs were jolted off the engine cylinders. As we didn't have any spares, this meant a thorough search under the floorboards of the cabin and perhaps pulling up every board both fore and aft.

We all got down on our knees and started searching. I looked at the sump. "They wouldn't have fallen in there, would they, Dad?" I asked.

"Put your hand in and find out," he suggested.

I looked at the dirty, oily sump and wondered how I would ever get all that mess off my hands and from under my fingernails before going to the picture-show.

Dad noticed my hesitation. "You've about fifteen minutes left," he remarked.

I plunged my hand right into the sump and felt around. The springs weren't there. I dried my hands on a dirty oil rag and started prising up the cabin floorboards. My sister was searching aft.

We searched for another ten minutes, but we couldn't find the springs anywhere. However, we were still afloat. Dad started scratching his head, which was a sign that his calculation had gone wrong somewhere, but he could find no logical reason for it. Those springs just had to be somewhere on the boat.

My younger sister stopped peering into the oily water beneath the boards and sat up. "Just what are we looking for?" she asked Dad.

Dad was fast losing his patience. He drew his fingers out of the oily bilge and drew a diagram for her on the floorboards. "Springs that look like that," he said. "There are two missing. They must be here somewhere. They fit on top here and we can't move without them."

"Oh, is that what you're looking for?" she said. "Here they are. I picked them up when we first hit the bank. Didn't know they were what you wanted."

Dad carefully controlled his temper and his tongue. He reached over, took the springs and put them back into place. My elder sister and I started replacing the floorboards. We didn't speak. Sometimes it was better to keep silent; this seemed one of those times.

We were quickly on our way again. My elder sister kept to the channel and steered the long way home. I sat and studied my dirty hands and fingernails while I tried to keep warm.

As we entered the gutter in front of our house, my father informed us he was not taking the boat right in, but would leave her in the channel. He had another trip to make that night. This meant we had to pick up the moored dinghy and use it to get ashore. Dad took over the tiller from my sister, told her to stand by the engine, and ordered me to stand by to jump from the boat into the dinghy as we came alongside it.

I hated doing that. My sisters made a much better job of jumping and picking up the dinghy than I did, and Dad knew it. He was obviously determined to teach me the art of jumping, in spite of my fears.

He signalled to my sister to cut the engine speed and nodded his head at me. My sister was a bit slow to act on the engine, and the boat was moving too fast, in my estimation, for me to make the jump. Fully expecting my father to take the boat round again for another try, I was astounded when he cracked out the command, "*Jump!*"

I obeyed instinctively, as he knew I would, because he had taught us to obey sudden, sharp commands without hesitation. My feet landed in the dinghy, but my body was pointing itself towards the water. I found myself clutching at the side of the dinghy, my feet reaching for the sky and my bottom over the side of the dinghy in the freezing cold water. I could hear my sisters laughing loudly as I struggled to get back into the dinghy with what was left of my dignity.

As I brought the dinghy alongside the boat—now anchored—my father looked ashore and saw my mother standing in the doorway of our house, awaiting our arrival. Then he looked at me.

"Girlie," he said very quietly, patiently and evenly, "when next you jump from a moving boat into an anchored dinghy, try facing the way the moving boat is going. You'll do a much better job that way."

I made a mental note of his advice. But I didn't thank him.

When we got ashore, Mother told us the picture-show had been cancelled; the film container had been left on the wharf at the mainland by mistake.

We all came to the conclusion it just was not our day.

Dugong Coming!

OLD Sammy of Myora was the catcher of dugong. Myora, years ago, was an Aboriginal mission station on Stradbroke Island, and some Aborigines were placed under what was known then as the "protective custody" of the missionaries. These missionaries were sent from the mainland; usually they were volunteers who believed that the Aborigine was in need of their Christian guidance. Each time a new missionary arrived at Myora, he would be of a different denomination from his predecessor, and once a student of Buddhism arrived. We children would follow him into the bush, where he would hide little carved idols in the branches of the trees. The white man called the place Myora, probably because he had misinterpreted the Aboriginal name, which is Moongalba.

At the first sign of the arrival of the dugong, Sammy would take his nets out into Moreton Bay. During the month of July the dugong came into the bay to suckle their young and wait for them to grow strong before taking them out into the Pacific Ocean. Dugong feed on seaweed, and when the chewed pieces of weed floated to the surface and were washed ashore by the incoming tide, we knew the dugong had once again taken up residence in the bay.

The dugong is a mammal. It has two hearts which are joined together, and it is able to stay alive in the sea as well as on land. It is a large creature, very much like a seal. It has, too, another name: it is often called the sea-cow. The flesh is a great delicacy, and was part of the staple diet of the Aborigines.

When Sammy visited the set nets to see if he had caught a dugong, we children always played on the hills to watch for his return. If a white shirt flapped from the mast of his boat, we knew he had been successful. Then our job was to alert the tribe and let them know a dugong had been caught. As soon as we saw the shirt waving in the breeze, we would scatter in all directions calling out to the women, "Dugong coming!"

The women would stop whatever they were doing, grab their dilly-bags and sugar-bags, and take off for the cutting-up and sharing-out place at Myora.

By the time all the tribe had assembled, the dugong would be lying on the sand at the foot of Gapembah Hill. The kids would be teasing each other and yelling their heads off, while the women gossiped in the shade of the big mango-tree. The men would be grouped around the dugong, and Sammy would be instructing them where to place it ready for the cutting-up.

The sharing-out of the flesh was simple. Each family was given sufficient to feed his own. If a man had ten children, he received a larger portion than a man with two. This is the Aboriginal way of sharing, according to the size of a family.

My mother had seven children and was always happy when Sammy threw into her bag part of the grumpii—the intestines. She would take home the precious meat, trusting us to help her with the heavy load, but she always carried the grumpii herself. I think she felt we might lose it.

As soon as we arrived home, she would light up the wood stove and then prepare the meat for cooking. Dugong meat looks very like beef, and Mother would roast it in the oven. She would wash the grumpii thoroughly in salt sea-water, then place it in a pot of water to boil on the stove until it was tender. After that it was allowed to cool while Mother minced up some of the flesh, and the heart and liver. This was all pushed into the grumpii, and the ends tied tightly with string, and it was then put into a pot of water once more and boiled. We called it grumpii sausage. In later years I had the opportunity to taste Scots haggis, and found it not unlike our dugong sausage. I enjoyed the taste of haggis as much as I liked our grumpii.

Today, when the white man's food is eaten so widely by Aborigines, the tribe no longer hunts the dugong. They believe that to hunt dugong when their bellies are full would be to act against the natural law of "kill to eat". They believe that the Good Spirit would punish them severely if they killed dugong out of greed—and that the Good Spirit might take one of the tribespeople to even the score.

The dugong still feed in Moreton Bay, and I am sure they must wonder what has become of their enemy, the black man. Sometimes, in July, when I see the chewed weed floating ashore on the high tide, my mouth waters for the taste of dugong. But the law of the tribe is good, and no one intends to break it just because of a longing for what used to be.

Stories from the
Old and New Dreamtime

The Beginning of Life

IN the Dreamtime all the earth lay sleeping. Nothing grew. Nothing moved. Everything was quiet and still. The animals, birds and reptiles lay sleeping under the earth's crust.

Then one day the Rainbow Serpent awoke from her slumber and pushed her way through the earth's crust, moving the stones that lay in her way. When she emerged, she looked about her and then travelled over the land, going in all directions. She travelled far and wide, and when she grew tired she curled herself into a heap and slept. Upon the earth she left her winding tracks and the imprint of her sleeping body. When she had travelled all the earth, she returned to the place where she had first appeared and called to the frogs, "Come out!"

The frogs were very slow to come from below the earth's crust, for their bellies were heavy with water which they had stored in their sleep. The Rainbow Serpent tickled their stomachs, and when the frogs laughed, the water ran all over the earth to fill the tracks of the Rainbow Serpent's wanderings—and that is how the lakes and rivers were formed.

Then grass began to grow, and trees sprang up, and so life began on earth.

All the animals, birds and reptiles awoke and followed the Rainbow Serpent, the Mother of Life, across the land. They were happy on the earth, and each lived and hunted for food with his own tribe. The kangaroo, wallaby and emu tribes lived on the plains. The reptile tribes lived among the rocks and stones, and the bird tribes flew through the air and lived in the trees.

The Rainbow Serpent made laws that all were asked to obey, but some grew quarrelsome and were troublemakers. The Rainbow Serpent scolded them, saying, "Those who keep my laws I shall reward well. I shall give to them a human form. They and their children and their children's children shall roam this earth for ever. This shall be their land. Those who break my laws I shall punish. They shall be turned to stone, never to walk the earth again."

So the law-breakers were turned to stone, and became mountains and hills, to stand for ever and watch over the tribes hunting for food at their feet.

But those who kept her laws she turned into human form, and gave each of them his own totem of the animal, bird or reptile whence they came. So the tribes knew themselves by their own totems: the kangaroo, the emu, the carpet snake, and many, many more. And in order that none should starve, she ruled that no man should eat of his own totem, but only of other totems. In this way there was food for all.

So the tribes lived together in the land given to them by the Mother of Life, the Rainbow Serpent; and they knew that the land would always be theirs, and that no one should ever take it from them.

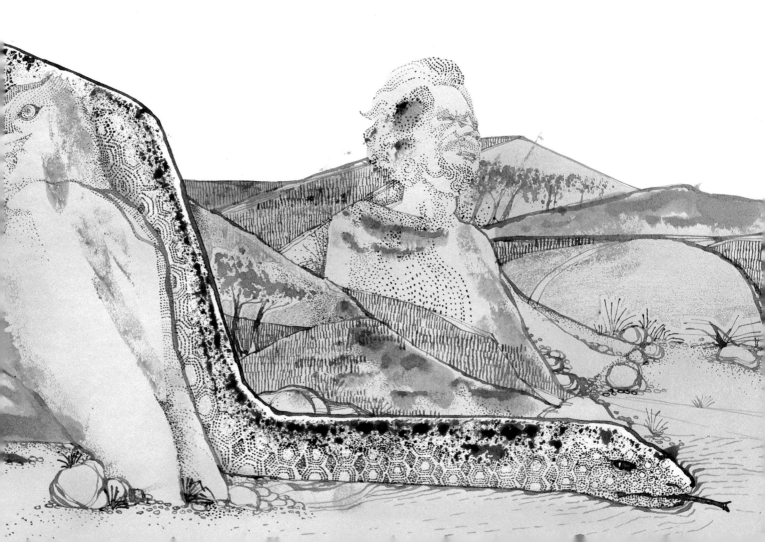

Biami and Bunyip

BIAMI was one of the wisest men whom the Rainbow Serpent created at the beginning of time, and when he grew old, the Mother of Life gave him a spirit form and the power to protect the tribes from harm. As Biami the Good Spirit he lived among the tribes and was much loved.

Now there was one tribesman who disobeyed the rule laid down by the Rainbow Serpent, and ate of his own totem animal. This made Biami very angry. At this time the Rainbow Serpent was sleeping in the place whence she came, below the earth, so Biami himself punished the wrongdoer by banishing him from the tribe. This man too took a spirit form upon himself, but he became an evil spirit. He was known as Bunyip. Biami warned the tribes to have nothing to do with Bunyip.

Bunyip was stirred with a deep anger; he vowed he would use his evil influence to bring unhappiness to the tribes. He made his home in the deep waterholes and the rain forests, lurking in the gloom by day and roaming the earth by night, during the time of darkness. He brought fear to the tribes, threatening to devour any human he might meet. The tribes called loudly upon Biami, asking him to protect them from Bunyip.

Some of the young women of the tribes foolishly disobeyed the elders, who had told them they must have nothing to do with Bunyip. They went to find Bunyip to test his evil power. Bunyip lay in wait for the women, and when they were close enough to fall into his power, he trapped them and made them his slaves. They lived with him as water spirits, and were lost to the tribes for ever. The elders discovered what had happened, and warned the tribes that these water spirits were being used by Bunyip to lure men into the black waters of Bunyip's gunyah, his home. So the tribes learnt to fear the water spirits, too.

These water spirits who had once been women of the tribes were lithe and lovely, and very evil. When a hunter drew near they would sing songs of love, and the hunter, hearing their beautiful voices, would seek them out. The water spirits would lead him on until he came at last to the place of dark waters where none of the tribe would venture by day or night. Then, when the evil power was strong upon the hunter, the water spirits would show themselves upon the water. "Follow, follow," they would call—and the hunter, overjoyed to see such beauty, would obey. He followed the spirits into the swamp and was drowned.

Even today, Bunyip still roams the evil waters and rain forests of the land.

Mirrabooka

(Southern Cross)

BIAMI the Good Spirit was kept very busy, guarding the tribes as they roamed throughout the earth, and he was much troubled for them. He found that he could not watch over all of them at once; he knew he must have help to keep them from harm.

Among the tribes there was a man called Mirrabooka, who was much loved for his wisdom, and the way in which he looked after the welfare of his people. Biami was well pleased with Mirrabooka, and when he grew old, Biami gave him a spirit form and placed him in the sky among the stars, and promised him eternal life. Biami gave Mirrabooka lights for his hands and feet and stretched him across the sky, so that he could watch for ever over the tribes he loved. And the tribes could look up to him from the earth and see the stars which were Mirrabooka's eyes gazing down on them.

When in later times white invaders came from across the sea and stole the tribal lands, they did not know that this group of stars across the southern sky was Mirrabooka, and they renamed them. They called Mirrabooka by the name of the Southern Cross. And the eyes of Mirrabooka they called the Pointers. But it is really Mirrabooka there, stretched across the sky; he will be there for ever, for Biami has made it so.

47

The Midden

AFTER the Rainbow Serpent had created the tribes, the food-gatherers went out every day at early light, walking many miles to find food to bring back to the camps. The women and children dug for yams and lily roots and hunted sand lizards and witchety grubs. The men went out with spears into the bush and across the plains, or launched their canoes to gather the larger food. Sometimes, they would break a tree branch beside a waterhole and move silently towards the ducks swimming on the water. When they got close enough, they would pull a duck out of the water by its feet. Before the startled bird had time to call out, its neck would be wrung and it would be hung on the belt tied round the hunter's waist. This belt was woven from the hair of the women, wound together with vine tendrils, or else from strips of kangaroo, wallaby or possum skin.

Sometimes the women would follow the tracks of smaller animals such as the possum to its sleeping-place. For the possum sleeps by day, and is easy prey for the wise hunter. The flying-fox, too, sleeps away the daylight, hanging upside-down—and it, too, is easy prey.

When the sun was low in the western sky, the hunters returned to camp with their day's catch. Burning fires welcomed them home. The smell of roasting flesh made their mouths water hungrily; the children would wait impatiently for their share of the food. When everyone had eaten and bellies were full, the bones and shells that were left were gathered together carefully and placed on top of each other. This was a law that they must all obey. If they were careless and scattered the bones and shells, then Biami the Good Spirit would punish them by scattering the living animals and fish, so that when the hunters went out next day, they would find it difficult to gather any food at all.

When the white man came to the land, he saw the middens that had been left by the tribal eating-places, and could not understand why the bones and shells should be so neatly stacked together. But every Aborigine knew that this was the rule of Biami, and that to keep their bellies filled they must obey that rule. For Biami the Good Spirit was interpreting the laws of the Rainbow Serpent, the Mother of Life, asleep within the ancient rocks of Australia.

Burr~Nong

(Bora Ring)

THE time of learning in the Aboriginal world never stops. It goes on and on. As soon as the children are able to sit up, they are taught to observe the reptiles, animals and birds and to draw them in the sand. In this way they learn to recognize every creature of the bush. And they learn, too, how to imitate their calls and cries.

The most exciting period of learning comes when the children are about twelve years old. At this time they learn the lessons from within the Burr-Nong ring. It is a period of testing, and they go on with it until they have passed every test—when they are between sixteen and eighteen. After they have passed out of the Burr-Nong, they are called men and women of the tribe.

During the Burr-Nong training the boys are handed over to the men of the tribe, and the girls to the women. They are taught the tribal secrets, and the art of manhood and womanhood. No woman may witness the Burr-Nong ceremony of the boys, and no man may see the Burr-Nong ceremony of the girls.

The boys are taught the tribal legends and must learn them by heart; for the Aborigines had no written language, and could not record their stories except in their hearts and minds. The children are also taught patience and tolerance, and the art of pain-bearing. No child is allowed to think of himself as being cleverer than another. If any child boasts of his ability during the Burr-Nong training, he would be severely punished by the tribal elders. No child is more important than another; they must all help each other to pass the tests.

The cutting of the Burr-Nong marks in their flesh teaches them to bear pain, as well as symbolizing their manhood and womanhood. If a hunter were far away from his tribe and fell ill, then the art of pain-bearing which he learnt in the Burr-Nong enables him to return to his camp fires in spite of the pain he may be suffering. The Rainbow Serpent, the Mother of Life, who laid down these rules for the tribes, taught her people well, how to live and find happiness in a harsh land.

No one in the tribe is given complete power over others in life. The welfare of the tribe is in the hands of a Council of Wise Men, the tribal elders. For Biami taught that wisdom comes with old age, and the aged feel less desire for selfish, individual power.

NOTE: *Burr-Nong rings are made of raised earth, and are perfectly round; there are sometimes two, sometimes three. Each tribal group has a different method of learning. Most are based on their environment. The Burr-Nong ring in the drawing belongs to the tribal groups that inhabited the east in and around Brisbane, Queensland. The link between the second and third rings is called the sacred way. This, too, is made of raised earth. In the last ring, the boys' Burr-Nong, the elders erect a platform made out of the upturned roots of a wattle-tree. When the final lesson is over in this third ring, the elders climb onto the platform and the young men take hold of the trunk of the tree and shake the old men down onto the ground. This is a symbolic gesture which means "Down with the old and up with the new hunters".*

Wonga and Nuda

WONGA and Nudu lived in the bush with their tribe. They were both about eight years old. Every day they went out with the women, for they were supposed to help gather food for the evening meal. They were a mischievous pair, those two boys, and the women found it difficult to keep their eyes on them when they went hunting.

One day Wonga and Nudu set out as usual to help the women gather small lizards, grubs, and lily roots. They dug out a few small lizards, and Nudu let one crawl away so that they could both watch him. He and Wonga studied the creature's footprints in the sand, then watched as he climbed a tree, looking at the scratch-marks he made. They had been taught to do this; it was part of the knowledge they needed to live in the bush.

Soon the two boys grew tired of helping the women. They waited until they were busy in the lagoon, gathering lily roots, then went off into the bush to play. They each had a small, blunt spear, and they pretended they were in a tribal fight, just like their elders. Wonga threw his spear first, and Nudu had to dodge and weave so that the spear would miss him. When Wonga did hit him, it was Nudu's turn to throw his spear. They always aimed at each other's feet, as they had been taught. It was a good way to learn the art of spear-throwing without getting hurt.

"Let's find old Duruk!" Wonga said suddenly. So they set off to find grumpy old Duruk the Emu, out on the plains. The bird raised his head as the two boys came by, listening to find out if their elders were close at hand. He did not run away from Wonga and Nudu; he knew it was only their hunting elders he need fear.

"Hullo, old Duruk!" the boys called.

"Duruk, duruk," grunted Emu as he raised his head to the wind.

Suddenly, he was off with the speed of the wind. His keen sense had caught the smell of the hunter. Three men of the tribe came out of the bushes, waving their spears, their beards bristling with anger. They shouted to Wonga and Nudu to get back to the women and not to frighten their game away.

The boys grabbed their spears and fled. When they had left the hunters far behind, they sat down and laughed at what they had done. They stretched out under an old gum-tree, and Nudu's sharp eyes discovered a kookaburra, sitting half-asleep on a branch.

"There's Goo-gee-gaar-gaar," he told Wonga.

"Hullo, Goo-gee-gaar-gaar," called Wonga.

Goo-gee-gaar-gaar was not afraid of the tribespeople. He knew the Aborigine called him brother and friend. They liked his laughter, and never killed his kind for food.

The two boys mimicked the bird's laughter, inviting him to laugh with them. But the kookaburra had just finished a meal of tree-snake, and was far too lazy and contented to perform, so they left him and went on.

Now they began to feel hungry, so they looked for a rotting tree stump, and when they had found one, began to explore the inside. Digging away with sticks, they soon found plenty of grubs, which they ate laughing with excitement. Their bellies satisfied, they went farther into the bush, watching at intervals the trail of the sun, for they knew they had to get back to the women before the hunting party left the lagoon for their camp. Brother Sun always told them when it was time to stop playing in the bush.

Wonga and Nudu knew every bird and animal in the bush. There was only one thing they feared: Bunyip the Evil Spirit. Their elders had warned them about Bunyip, telling them how he would lie in wait for the little children of the tribe. If he caught one, he would take him away to the deep, dark waterhole where he lived. The boys did not know exactly where Bunyip's home was; they believed it was somewhere far away. They always looked very carefully about them in case Bunyip was near. They knew he could turn himself into any form to trick the children of the tribe. They felt glad that Biami the Good Spirit was always close at hand to protect them, and that brother Sun shone brightly in the sky. For they knew Bunyip did not like bright sunlight. He liked dark, wet, cloudy days—and the dark night, when he could stalk about without being seen.

Now brother Sun was watching Wonga and Nudu as they strayed farther and farther from the women at the lagoon. He decided to teach them a lesson, and so he hid behind a huge black cloud in the sky.

Wonga and Nudu stopped their laughing and talking and looked up at the sky, calling to Sun to come out from behind the cloud. But the sun did not come out. When the boys saw the dark cloud shadows spreading over the bush, they were frightened. Suddenly a loud noise came from the undergrowth a short distance away. There was a thumping and thrashing: the boys, terrified, picked up their spears and ran as fast as they could to the lagoon. As they ran, the noise pursued them, but they were too frightened to look behind.

"It's Bunyip! Run, run!" Nudu shouted.

Wonga ran as fast as Nudu. Sun looked round the edge of the black cloud in the sky and smiled. Soon the boys came to where the women were gathering up their dilly-bags, ready to return to the camp. When they saw Wonga and Nudu, they scolded them for running away. They should have been gathering the food instead of playing. Wonga and Nudu were out of breath, but they managed to gasp out their tale of Bunyip.

"We heard him thump, thump, thumping and thrashing behind us!" Wonga told them.

The women looked up at the sky, where the sun had appeared once more. They smiled wisely. They knew what had happened, but they did not tell Wonga and Nudu that Sun had played a trick on them. He had sent wallaby to jump and crash through the bush and chase the boys back to the lagoon.

Wonga and Nudu stayed close beside the women as they made their way home. They thought that Sun had chased Bunyip away. They looked up at him and smiled their thanks for his protection as their weary legs walked the long distance home to the camp fires of their tribe.

Curlew

CURLEW was a tribe that stayed close to mother earth, and carefully guarded its own people. They never slept by night, but stayed awake to give the warning cry should danger come near those they loved. When the tribes heard Curlew's cry in the night, they knew some danger was present. They feared the cry, yet they loved Curlew for his watchfulness. He was a true brother to them.

One day Biami the Good Spirit called Curlew before him and said, "Your love for your tribe shall be rewarded. Tell me how."

Curlew replied, "Turn me and my people into birds. Give us wings so that we may fly, and let us be the guardians of the departed ones. Allow us to warn the tribes when death is at hand. We shall come to warn three times, when darkness lies over the land. We shall carry the shades of the dead to the shadow land. Our tribal brothers will be less afraid if we fly with them when the time comes for their last journey."

Biami saw the wisdom of Curlew's words, so he granted the request he had made. And now Curlew carries to the shadow land the shades of men who have departed this life. First, he gives warning three times, so that the tribes will know he is coming, and will not be afraid. Curlew's cry tells the tribes that all is well for their loved ones in death, that they are not alone. They know that their blood-brother, Curlew, will always be with them when they make their last journey.

Oodgeroo

(Paperbark-tree)

IN the new Dreamtime there lived a woman, an Aborigine, who longed for her lost tribe, and for the stories that had belonged to her people; for she could remember only the happenings of her own Dreamtime. But the old Dreamtime had stolen the stories and hidden them. The woman knew that she must search for the old stories—and through them she might find her tribe again.

Before she set off, she looked for her yam-stick and dilly-bag, but Time had stolen these, too. She found a sugar-bag that the ants had left and which Time had forgotten to destroy, and she picked it up and carried it with her wherever she went. Time laughed at her efforts; he thought her new dilly-bag was useless.

One day, as she searched, the woman came upon the ashes of a fire her own tribe had kindled long ago. Tears came to her eyes, for she yearned for her tribe, and felt lonely. She sat down by the ashes and ran her fingers through the remains of the fire that had once glowed there. And as she looked at the ashes, she called to Biami the Good Spirit to help her find her tribe.

Biami told her to go to the paperbark-trees and ask them to give her some of their bark. The paperbark-trees loved this woman who had lost her tribe, and they gave her their bark. They knew she was not greedy and would not take more than she needed. So she put the bark in her dilly-bag.

Then Biami told the woman to return to the dead fire of her tribe, collect all the charred sticks, and place these, too, in her bag—and to do this each time she came upon the dead fire of any lost tribe.

Time did not understand what the woman was doing, so he followed her.

She travelled far and wide over the earth, and each time she came upon the dead fire of a lost tribe, she would gather the charred sticks, and when at last her bag was filled with them, she went to the secret dreaming-places of the old tribes. Here she rested and again called to Biami, and asked him to help her remember the old stories, so that through them she might find her tribe.

Biami loved this woman, and he put into her mind a new way in which she might find those stories and her tribe. The woman sat down and drew from her bag the charred pieces of stick she had taken from the dead fires, and placed the paperbark flat upon the ground. She drew the sticks across the paperbark, and saw that they made marks on its surface.

So she sat for many years, marking the paperbark with the stories of the long-lost tribes, until she had used up all the charred remnants she had gathered and her bag was empty. In this way she recalled the stories of the old Dreamtime, and through them entered into the old life of the tribes.

And when next the paperbark-trees filled the air with the scent of their sweet, honey-smelling flowers, they took her into their tribe as one of their own, so that she would never again be without the paperbark she needed for her work. They called her Oodgeroo. And this is the story of how Oodgeroo found her way back into the old Dreamtime. Now she is happy, because she can always talk with the tribes whenever she wants to. Time has lost his power over her because Biami has made it so.

Tuggan-Tuggan

(Silky Oak)

TUGGAN-TUGGAN was a hunter of the Moreton Bay tribe. One day, as he was searching for food, armed with his boomerang, he came across a slender and very beautiful tree. Tuggan-Tuggan fell in love with the beautiful tree. He felt that the tree was unhappy, and asked her what was the matter.

The tree shook her silvery-green leaves in the wind and told him how she wished she had a cloak to cover her trembling leaves to keep them warm. Tuggan-Tuggan promised to help her. Every day he searched for a cloak to cover the beautiful tree, instead of hunting for food.

The elders of the tribe grew angry with Tuggan-Tuggan when he returned each day empty-handed from the hunt. At last they told him that if he did not bring food to the tribe, he would be punished. But Tuggan-Tuggan took no notice, and went on searching for a cloak for his lovely, sad tree. And one day the elders decided it was time for his punishment.

When Tuggan-Tuggan next returned to the camp, they took his boomerang from him and threw it high in the air. They told Tuggan-Tuggan that since he did not use his boomerang any more for hunting, he did not need it, and now it would never return to the camp. And they told him that he, too, must go away and not return.

Tuggan-Tuggan watched his boomerang travelling fast out of sight, and made up his mind that he would follow its path until he found it again. For he loved his boomerang as much as he loved that tall, cold tree. He travelled all over the land looking everywhere for his lost boomerang, and searching as he went for a cloak for the shivering tree. His travels took him far away. But he could not hunt for himself without his boomerang, and without meat he grew sick and weary and lost his strength. He stumbled back the long way he had come, and when at last he reached his beautiful tree once more, he knew that he was dying.

Now Biami the Good Spirit knew of Tuggan-Tuggan's love for the tree, and in pity he found and returned Tuggan-Tuggan's boomerang to him. Dying, Tuggan-Tuggan told the tree: "This is the last time I shall ever use my boomerang. Since I could not find a cloak for you, I shall throw my boomerang into the highest of your branches. It will keep you warm and make you happy."

And when he threw his boomerang, it circled the tree and touched the shivering green leaves, then broke into a thousand golden pieces that covered all the branches. So the boomerang formed a golden cloak for the tree, which has been warm and happy ever since. And Tuggan-Tuggan died fulfilling his wish.

Talwalpin and Kowinka

(Cotton-tree and Red Mangrove)

TALWALPIN was a beautiful woman of the tribe. She was tall and strong and loved to wear, twisted in her hair, the yellow flowers that grew everywhere. She wore them even when she was asleep. Kowinka was a young hunter who loved Talwalpin. He guarded Talwalpin while she slept, smiling at the bright-yellow flowers in her hair.

Talwalpin and Kowinka spent many happy times together in Kowinka's canoe. Kowinka would paddle the big canoe to a place where there were many fish, and the tribe always had plenty of fish to eat when Talwalpin and Kowinka went hunting.

Now Talwalpin could not swim, but she was never afraid when she went fishing in the canoe, for Kowinka was the greatest swimmer of the tribe. One day, when they were out in the canoe, a big storm blew up. Kowinka got out his paddle and turned the canoe towards the shore. But, in spite of his strong, fast strokes, the wind kept blowing the canoe farther and farther out to sea. Their tribe, standing on the beach, cried for Talwalpin and Kowinka to come back, but the wind was strong and Kowinka was growing weak. Talwalpin took up another paddle, and together they fought the storm. Sometimes they would come close to the shore, then the wind would hurl the canoe into the waves and blow them out to sea again.

The tribal elders told the young men to take out their canoes and rescue Talwalpin, for they knew that she could not swim. When the young men came close to Kowinka's canoe, they called for Talwalpin to jump so that they could rescue her, but she would not leave Kowinka, and so the young men returned to the shore.

Soon Talwalpin and Kowinka were too exhausted to fight the storm any longer. Kowinka jumped into the sea and tried to pull the canoe to shore, but a huge wave overturned the canoe, and they were both drowned.

Biami the Good Spirit took pity on Talwalpin and Kowinka, and placed their shades close together. In the morning, when the storm had gone far out to sea, the tribe found Talwalpin washed up on the sand, and Kowinka in the water, floating near by.

Now Talwalpin grows in the sand, the beautiful cotton-tree with her bright-yellow flowers still in her hair. And Kowinka, the red mangrove, stands with his feet in the water, guarding Talwalpin for ever. These two always grow side by side: one on the bank and the other in the water. Their love is so strong that they can never leave one another.

Pomera

(Banksia)

P OMERA, the hunter, loved a beautiful woman of the tribe, but she had been given to another. No one knew of Pomera's secret love for this forbidden woman. When Pomera went hunting, he plotted how he could take the woman for his own. He was a great hunter, much admired by the tribe for his skill at bringing down the game. He always brought home to the camp fires the largest animals of all.

One day, when the food was cooked, Pomera was invited to choose the part he wanted most before it was shared out between all the other members of the tribe. But instead of selecting the part he wanted, Pomera shocked all the tribe by demanding that the woman he loved should be given to him. His boldness made the elders very angry. They refused to listen to his demand, and told him again to choose the best part of the meat, according to the custom of the tribe. But Pomera was proud, and he grew angry too. He refused the meat and went off by himself. He no longer hunted with the tribe.

One day, alone in the forest, he made a plan to outwit the elders and steal the woman. Secretly he made a nulla-nulla, a hunting-club, carving great knobs on it. Then he covered it with feathers, so that no one could tell it was a nulla-nulla.

It was not long before he came upon the woman alone at the waterhole. Carrying his nulla-nulla, he approached her. She had no fear of him, because she thought all he was carrying was a branch covered with cream flowers. Then Pomera raised the nulla-nulla, struck the woman on the head, and carried her off. But the blow from the great knobby nulla-nulla crushed the woman's head, and when at last Pomera placed her on the ground, far away from the tribal ground, she was dead.

Pomera had left his nulla-nulla by the waterhole, and when the elders found it there, they knew what had happened, and called to Biami the Good Spirit to punish Pomera.

So Biami turned Pomera into a tree, and covered him with creamy flowers that looked like those he had made from feathers to cover his nulla-nulla. Each year the birds of the air come screeching to pick off the flowers that cover the tree, and when the flowers have all gone, then the round, knobbed nulla-nulla that Pomera made can be seen all over the tree. So the tribe can never forget Pomera's treachery and his love for a forbidden woman, and as a tree he must carry his shame for ever.

Tia-Gam

(Lawyer Vine)

TIA-GAM was a happy child who loved to tease. He would throw water on the fires when no one was looking, so that the smoke would rise and sting the eyes of the tribe. He would hide the women's dilly-bags, so that they would waste much time searching for them before they could go off to gather the lily roots and shellfish. He would tangle the men's nets so that they could not fish. He would tease the other children, tripping them as they ran past. And whenever his tricks caused discomfort, he would laugh to himself and think how clever he was.

Tia-Gam made the tribe very cross and he was often scolded, but never smacked or struck, for that was not the way of the tribe. The tribal elders lost patience with him many times, but no one wanted to see him punished, because in spite of all his tricks and teasing everyone loved him. The other children laughed with him at his jokes, and the women made excuses for his naughty ways. When the tribal elders met together to make a plan to teach Tia-Gam a lesson, they could not think of any way to do this. So Tia-Gam went on teasing and playing tricks. He knew very well how fond of him the rest of the tribe was; he thought he could do anything he liked.

Tia-Gam often went off by himself, away from the women whose duty it was to look after him. Then the hunters would scold the women for not looking after him as they should. One day Tia-Gam wandered off by himself into the dark, damp rain forest. He knew that it was forbidden to go there, but he did not care.

Now Bunyip lived in the rain forest—and Bunyip was the Evil Spirit. As Tia-Gam wandered in the forest, he saw Bunyip, but he did not know it was Bunyip, because Bunyip could change himself into many forms. Tia-Gam thought he was a hunter of the tribe. Bunyip was worried because Sun was getting through the branches of the tall trees in his rain forest and bringing light to it. He did not want Sun to enter his rain forest. When Bunyip saw Tia-Gam, he called to him and asked him to climb the tall trees and weave their branches closer together.

Tia-Gam was very pleased. This hunter must think he was a very clever climber to ask him to do this. He climbed to the tops of the trees, and joined the branches together so tightly that Sun could not get through.

When Bunyip saw what a good climber Tia-Gam was, he cast a spell upon him, and Tia-Gam became his slave and stayed in the dark, damp rain forest for ever. He is there still; Bunyip will never let him go. Now Tia-Gam spends his time going from tree to tree, up and down the tall trunks and across the ground between them, always searching for a way back to the tribe he left behind him. And still, in the rain forest, he plays mischievous tricks, for when the birds and animals and hunters cross his path, he tries to trip them and make them fall to the ground. The children of his tribe know he is there, still playing tricks, and they are sad because Bunyip will never let him return to them.

Boonah

(Bloodwood Gum)

BOONAH was a hunter of a Brisbane tribe that lived at the foot of a mountain. His tribe were artists, who delighted in making pictures. All the other tribes admired them, for they were peace-makers. They brought peace and happiness wherever they went. They spent their time solving the problems of the other tribes. They intervened in quarrels so that peace was restored. They stood tall and straight and their fingers were long and slender.

Now on the top of the mountain there lived another tribe. They were lazy and quarrelsome and had been banished to live apart from the other tribes. So they had gone to the top of the mountain, where they lived alone with only Bunyip for company. For the mountain-top was Bunyip's rain-forest home.

The banished tribe blamed Boonah for their troubles, because he had talked against them at the tribal council meeting when they had been banished. They decided to seek their revenge on Boonah.

One day, as Boonah was hunting for food at the foot of the mountain, the banished tribe looked down and saw him, and decided to kill him. They picked up stones from the top of the mountain and threw them down on Boonah.

Now Bunyip did not like the banished ones living on the mountain, for they disturbed his rain-forest home, and he chose this moment to shake the mountain, so that a sudden avalanche of stones carried the banished tribe to their death. They turned to dust where they fell, at the foot of the mountain.

But Boonah's tribe, too, were caught by the avalanche, and Boonah himself was the first to be killed. The rocks, hurtling down, snapped his slender body and blood flowed from him. And after Boonah, all his tribe fell to the ground, dying, and their blood made the soil red.

Then Boonah and his tribe turned into trees, tall and slender, with long, thin green leaves that pointed to the ground to tell the story of their destruction. And when the other tribes came to the foot of the mountain, they read Boonah's message, and knew that the red gum on the slender trunks of the bloodwood-trees was the blood of Boonah's tribe.

Boonah still weeps tears of blood and still stands straight and strong. His slender leaves point downward for ever in memory of the quarrelsome tribe from the mountain-top, turned to dust at his feet.

Mai

(Black Bean)

MAI was the maker of flour which the women of her tribe used for the cakes they baked on the hot stones. She would travel far and wide looking for the seeds she pounded to make the flour.

One day, when Mai was out searching, she saw an old woman chattering and screeching to herself. Mai noticed that the old woman was carrying many seeds; she asked if she might have some of them. But the old woman was selfish and mean. She would never share with anyone outside her own tribe. All her tribe were like herself; and they did not gather their seeds, as Mai did, but stole them from the other tribes. They would paint themselves with many colours to blend with the surroundings, so that no one would see them when they came to steal.

Again Mai asked the old woman for some of her seeds, and again the old woman screeched at her and drove her away. Mai decided she would make a plan to punish the old woman. She watched where the old woman hid her seeds, and when she was asleep, Mai went to the place and took them away. Then she asked the honey ants to sit where the seeds had been.

When the old woman awoke and went to the place where she had left her seeds, she found the ants and became very angry. Screeching as loud as she could, she picked up the ants and bit them in half.

Then the ants punished both the old woman and Mai for stealing. They turned the old woman and all her many-coloured tribe into birds; and Mai they turned into a tree. Now, the old woman's tribe, still screeching, searches the blossoms of that tree for the lost seed which Mai stole from the old woman so long ago. And the flowers of the black-bean-tree are the same colours as the plumage of the mountain parrots that tear at them in their search for food.